COMBAT SCHIZOPHRENIA WITH THE MEGAVITAMIN AND NUTRITIONAL STRATEGIES OF ORTHOMOLECULAR PSYCHIATRY

Schizophrenia is a disease and syndrome with biochemical origins that has the hallmarks of debilitating perceptual disorders and thought disturbances. Orthomolecular psychiatry, a treatment strategy that uses megadoses of vitamins B-3 and C in conjunction with correct nutrition, yields a 90 percent recovery rate in acute cases and up to 50 percent in chronic patients. This guide by the cofounder of orthomolecular therapy offers a step-by-step approach so that patients and their families will get the maximum benefits from treatment.

A. Hoffer, M.D., Ph.D., is one of the founders of the field of orthomolecular medicine. His discovery that niacin lowers cholesterol is credited with the initiation of the paradigm in nutritional medicine that we now accept as standard, that vitamins are used for treatment and not just for prevention of deficiency disease. He was also one of the researchers who discovered that megadoses of vitamin B-3 and ascorbic acid were therapeutic for schizophrenia, the premise that remains at the heart of orthomolecular psychiatry as it is practiced today. Dr. Hoffer is the editor-in-chief of the *Journal of Orthomolecular Medicine*. He is the author of several books about orthomolecular therapy and has over 500 published articles to his credit.

Orthomolecular Treatment for Schizophrenia

Megavitamin supplements and nutritional strategies for healing and recovery

by A. Hoffer, M.D., Ph.D., F.R.C.P. (C)

KEATS PUBLISHING

LOS ANGELES

NTC/Contemporary Publishing Group

Orthomolecular Treatment for Schizophrenia is intended solely for education and information and not as medical advice. Please consult a medical or health professional if you have any questions about your health.

Published by Keats, a division of NTC/Contemporary Publishing Group, Inc., 4255 West Touhy Avenue, Lincolnwood, Illinois 60646-1975 U.S.A.

International Stai.dard Book Number: 0-87983-910-4

22 23 24 25 26 27 QVS/QVS 24 23 22 21 20

Contents

On a pleasant mid-June Saturday afternoon in 1996, I attended my patient's graduation party. He had just received a B.A. in Psychology from the University of Victoria and was planning to do postgraduate work.[1]

What is remarkable about this young man's achievement is that four years earlier his family had been told by his psychiatrist that: (1) he would never get well, (2) he would never complete grade twelve, and (3) he would never get off tranquilizers. His father had been devastated by such a dismal prognosis, but his son was schizophrenic and tranquilizers were standard treatment. Had the boy remained in the care of that psychiatrist, it is likely that the doctor's predictions would have come true, since such is the fate of 90 percent of the early schizophrenic patients treated by drugs alone.

Fortunately, this patient was referred to me and started on the orthomolecular regimen. Today he is well. My definition of "well" is that a patient is free of symptoms, gets along with his family and community, and works or is preparing for work. Coincidentally, I have saved Canada $2 million, since this is what it costs the country to support the care of any schizophrenic who becomes ill, whether the person is treated with drugs or left untreated during the typical forty-year life span after the disease strikes.

At the party and my patient introduced me to his cousin, an educated woman with an M.A. in social work, who had been teaching and held responsible jobs, but had become schizophrenic three years earlier. She had been treated with electroconvulsive therapy (ECT) and was taking lithium, clozapine, and resperidal. She whispered to me that at least she was free of voices, but she could not drink her coffee without someone steadying her hand. She had severe tardive dyskinesia, a debilitating neuromuscular reaction that causes tremors and random movements of any muscle group. The medication she was taking made her obese, swollen with fluid from her ankles to her waist. She had so little energy that the exposure of a few hours to the tea party would force her to go to bed for three days, according to her mother, whose predictions proved accurate. No wonder the young woman was demoralized.

In December 1996, the young man and his parents came to see me to review his progress. He was halfway through a postgraduate course, after which he planned further study. He had gained self-confidence and was getting on well. The family then told me that the young woman I'd met had become so ill after the party she had to remain in bed for several weeks. However, after several months she asked her psychiatrist whether she could follow the same program that included megadoses of vitamin B-3 and vitamin C, as her cousin had. Her psychiatrist, who admitted that he had been unsuccessful in helping her during the three years they had worked together as patient and doctor, approved of her new regimen. She was hospitalized briefly but remained on the vitamin program and began to improve.

These two cases represent the two different treatment modalities. The standard treatment, drugs only, left both cousins gravely impaired and heading downhill. In contrast, using orthomolecular treatment, the male cousin, a patient considered by modern psychiatrists to be terminal in the sense that he would never recover, did recover. After a few months of treatment, the female cousin was also on the road to recovery. If they had not been treated by orthomolecular means, these patients would have never been able to live normal lives. Four years of drug therapy using tranquilizers did not work for either of them, but a few months of orthomolecular treatment created powerful, positive changes and set the stage for their return to wellness.

TERMINOLOGY: THE EVOLUTION OF "ORTHOMOLECULAR"

The term "orthomolecular" was used for the first time in 1968 by Linus Pauling[2] in his *Science* report called "Orthomolecular Psychiatry." This terminology was an improvement over the earlier phrase, "molecular" medicine, coined shortly after he had demonstrated that sickle-cell anemia is a molecular disease.[3] He showed that a genetic anomaly of the molecular structure of the hemoglobin was responsible for its tendency to change its shape into a sickled cell which could not traverse the capillaries, as did normal cells, under certain conditions. The conceptual distance traveled between "molecular" and "orthomolecular" was immense, according to Pauling, who now suggested that these molecular diseases could only be treated successfully by using orthomolecular methods.

"Ortho" means the "right" or the "best." This implies that to treat these molecular diseases properly, one needs to use molecules normally present in the body. No deficiency of any kind can be treated by anything other than that which replaces the specific deficiency. An excess of something can only be dealt with by removing that excess. An enzyme deficiency cannot be replaced by any drug. Pauling's work suggests that no molecular disease—no disease caused by some defect in the biochemical reactions in the body—will be cured by the use of xenobiotic molecules because, whether very valuable or very harmful, they are of limited use. This is why none of the drugs available today have ever been curative for any of the chronic diseases.

Orthomolecular therapy arose out of megavitamin therapy, and that's one of the main reasons it has been rejected for so long. We are witnessing a major battle of the paradigms, a shift in which the whole area of nutrition and nutritional medicine is being transformed from the accepted "vitamins-as-prevention" paradigm to the modern "vitamins-as-treatment" paradigm. As is common with all paradigm shifts, the defenders of the old do not like the vociferous proponents of the new and will use every resource at their command to block the new ideas. The new eventually wins acceptance, but it may take over four decades before a new paradigm is firmly established. The history of orthomolecular medicine is a history of this paradigm battle.[4]

VITAMINS-AS-PREVENTION

The vitamins-as-prevention paradigm was very useful in its day. It arose out of the observation that vitamins were needed in tiny amounts and only for a few classical deficiency diseases. Thus, vitamin B-1 would prevent beriberi, vitamin C would prevent scurvy, and so on. The isolation of these factors depended upon creating these deficiency diseases in animals and then restoring their health by giving them back what had been taken from their food. Initially this paradigm was resisted vigorously by the medical establishment, but it was finally accepted and in widespread practice by 1950. The years spanning 1935 to 1950 witnessed an amazing flowering of practice and theory using this paradigm and led to large-scale public health measures that included adding a few of these factors to our food: flour, apple juice, milk, and so on.

The underlying premises of this paradigm were firmly established in public policy, medical practice, and popular use. Essentially, they were reduced to the following ideas—as well known to some of us in the medical profession as the tenets of the Ten Commandments are to the general public. These are:

1. Thou shalt not use vitamins to treat anything which is not a classical deficiency disease.
2. Thou shalt not use megavitamin therapy.
3. Thou shalt use the holy Recommended Daily Allowances (RDAs).

Even though RDAs had not been extensively field-tested to prove their efficacy, belief in the utility of RDAs became firmly established in the medical community. Like any church, the vitamins-as-prevention paradigm severely punished its heretics—doctors who refused to obey its commandments have lost their licenses to practice medicine.

Even as this paradigm was being established, the seeds of its own destruction began to sprout. Chronic pellagrins did not recover with FDAs of vitamin B-3. Megavitamin doses of 600 mg daily were often needed to get relief.

In 1955, we published data to prove that niacin lowered cholesterol levels,[5] a finding confirmed shortly thereafter by the Mayo Clinic. Today, niacin is recognized as one of the most valuable, effective, and inexpensive substances for lowering cholesterol and elevating high density lipoprotein cholesterol. Our finding disobeyed both commandments. We used megadoses of a vitamin to treat a condition that is not a vitamin deficiency disease. The startling result is credited with being the beginning of the new paradigm—"vitamins-as-treatment." Thus our work actually instigated the major assault on the RDA paradigm.

VITAMINS-AS-TREATMENT

The modern paradigm, vitamins-as-treatment, acknowledges that many conditions not recognized as classical vitamin deficiency diseases can be treated by vitamins, and that one should use optimum doses, not the arbitrarily low doses of the RDAs. Different diseases, as well as different degrees of stress such as pregnancy and lactation, will have different optimum requirements. Perhaps we should have ODAs (Optimum Disease Allowances). These would serve as more useful guidelines but would also require a wider margin of dosages. The treatment of schizophrenia is a case in point—it represents a disease in which megadoses of vitamin B-3 must be used. The treatment of heart disease by megadoses of vitamin E represents another such condition. In fact, there are many nondeficiency diseases that respond to megavitamin therapy and can be defined as vitamin dependency diseases—those for which patients require much larger dosages of vitamins if they are to attain optimum health.

Fortunately, modern medicine is rapidly accepting the new paradigm; unfortunately, psychiatry is not. Modern psychiatry, seduced by the drug companies and their wares, has no use for nutrition nor for nutrients (these are not being promoted with huge advertising budgets, commercially motivated conferences, training sessions, etc.). When treatment is determined by a bottom-line mentality, the only profit that flows from drugs is the long-term, unsuccessful treatment of the chronically ill, a monetary profit of benefit to the industry, not the patient. We cannot forget that the business of business is to make money, but the business of medicine is to cure the sick.

WHAT IS SCHIZOPHRENIA?

THE SYMPTOMS

Schizophrenia is a mental disorder that involves two primary categories of symptoms: perceptual symptoms and thought disorder. Perceptual symptoms affect one or many of the senses (i.e., illusions and hallucinations such as voices, visions, and more often, subtle distortions of the visual world). Thought disorders refer to the inability to correctly judge the real world (i.e., paranoid thinking, ideas of reference, grandiosity, etc.), so that the person concludes that such perceptual changes are real and may or may not act upon them accordingly. Thus, if a person hears a voice telling him to burn down his neighbor's house, and if he does not realize the voice is created by his own sick brain, he may conclude that the voice must be coming from God. If he is a God-fearing person, he will obey and burn the house down. The neighbors will be totally amazed because, although they know what he has done, they do not know why. This leads to a lot of useless speculation about the "real" motives. Thus a shy, young person commits some heinous act. The neighbors rally round and say he was so quiet, so nice, polite, but reserved. They wonder why this could have happened. They do not realize that schizophrenia can so distort the personality of its victims that no matter how normal they were, they are no longer normal after the illness has struck.

SCHIZOPHRENIA DEFINED—A BRIEF HISTORY

The history of how schizophrenia has been defined is interesting and illustrates why there has been so much diagnostic confusion and inadequate treatment to date. Schizophrenia was first described about 200 years ago. By 1900 it was called "dementia praecox," which was later replaced by the term "schizophrenia," meaning a split: a schism between thinking and feeling. This concept has been interpreted to mean that there was a split personality. However, the idea of a split was wrong. The only split was the one that separated the patients from their families and the communities.

Definitions have changed. In England until 1900, schizophrenia was defined as a disease of perception combined with an inability to tell whether these perceptual changes were real or not. J. Conolly's book, *Indications of Insanity*,[6] provides the best and most accurate description of this disease. After 1900, Dr. E. Bleuler[7] confused the issue by emphasizing thought disorder and relegating perceptual changes to a minor status. This has become today's standard definition and is one reason for the extensive diagnostic confusion—schizophrenia has been confused with manic depressive disease (bipolar) and, more recently, with borderline personality disorders (BPD). If such diagnostic confusion could be eliminated, earlier diagnosis would be possible and treatment results would improve significantly.

In the United States, however, the diagnosis of schizophrenia had been more precise for twenty to thirty years and has included both sets of symptoms. Eventually, however, English psychiatrists convinced the Americans that they were too free and easy in their diagnosis and demanded that American physicians restrict the diagnosis of schizophrenia to deteriorated patients. All the others previously labeled schizophrenic were now to be classified as manic-depressive or any one of a number of new diagnoses invented by the creative genius of the APA diagnostic manual, the most recent version of which is *DSM-IV*.[8]

HOW DIAGNOSIS AFFECTS TREATMENT

At one time, the diagnosis determined what the treatment should be. Manic depressives were treated with lithium, schizophrenics were treated with one or more powerful tranquilizing drugs. Today, modern medicine tries to eliminate all traces of schizophrenia. The bias is such that if doctors detect any evidence of mood disorder, the patient is promptly relabeled manic-depressive and given lithium and if patients have prominent changes in personality, they are promptly declared untreatable and dismissed. It does not much matter what the diagnosis is because the treatment will be the same: any one of a number of tranquilizers and/ or antidepressants, psychotherapy, and perhaps for a lucky few, some support patiently given over many years.

I use the Conolly diagnostic definition.[6] Conolly defined insanity as a disease of perception combined with the inability to determine that the perceptual changes were false. Schizophrenia exists when perceptual symptoms are present, combined with thought disorder as described earlier. Unless patients tell you what their perceptual disturbances are and talk about how they react to them, it will be impossible to explain their behavior.

To illustrate, many years ago a clergyman was admitted to the psychiatric ward because he had been caught in the act of behaving inappropriately, chasing a young girl on the main street of a big city. He was very puzzled when he was forced to come to hospital. When I examined him and asked him what he had been doing, he said that while he was walking downtown in the late afternoon he suddenly saw the heavens open with a vast illumination from which he heard God tell him, "You have syphilis. You must have intercourse with a young virgin." He interpreted this command as an order from God and obediently began to chase the young girl. His visual and auditory experiences were the hallucinations. His determination that the words came from God was his delusion, and his behavior resulted from the combination of these two sets of symptoms. He was one of the first patients we treated with niacin. He recovered, remained well, and rose to a high position in the church.

DIAGNOSTIC TESTS TO DETECT SCHIZOPHRENIA

These symptoms are usually easily elicited by direct questions. There are two especially valuable and helpful diagnostic tests: the Hoffer Osmon Diagnostic (HOD)[9,10,11] and the Experiential World Inventory by El Meligi and Osmond,[12] which is more advanced and precise but takes more time to administer and to interpret. The Conolly description of schizophrenia is provided in our book, *How to Live with Schizophrenia*.

The Hoffer Osmond Diagnostic (HOD) test consists of 145 cards, each containing a statement on the front and a number on the back. The questions are designed so that the tester gets a view of the experiential world of the person being tested. The subject is instructed to read each card and to place the card in a True or False category—a process that takes, on average, between 10 and 20 minutes. The cards are recorded by their numbers on a scoring sheet. The pattern of the scores is assessed using templates, or more recently, by a computer program. Since the basis for the questions is the schizophrenic experience, it is not surprising that schizophrenic patients score very much higher than patients who are not schizophrenic or are normal. I have been using this test for thirty-five years, as have a few other physicians. Psychiatrists and psychologists prefer to use the MMPI (Minnesota Multiphasic Inventory), a test that, in my opinion, is useless in the diagnosis of most cases of schizophrenia. It is interesting that many chiropractors are skillfully using the HOD test now.

SCHIZOPHRENIA AS A SYNDROME

Having just described schizophrenia as a disease, I hasten to add that it is, in fact, not one disease, but a group of diseases: a syndrome. Several factors lead to the constellation of perceptual disturbances and thought disorder. Some of these factors are:

1. allergies known as cerebral allergies
2. vitamin B-3 and vitamin B-6 dependencies
3. vitamin deficiences such as scurvy or pellagra
4. essential fatty acid deficiencies
5. mineral deficiencies, such as zinc deficiency
6. toxic reactions to lead, for example, or to drugs
7. LSD and similar hallucinogens

8. infections such as rheumatic fever, syphilis, and many others

Let us now consider the first two: food allergic reactions and the vitamin dependencies.

Food Allergies

As obvious as this sounds, it must be stated unequivocally: It is essential to determine what is the cause of the syndrome. About half of the chronic patient population experience allergies to one or more foods. If the patient is schizophrenic due to daily milk consumption, giving him tranquilizers will control some of the symptoms but that person will not respond to vitamin therapy alone. There will be no cure until the dairy products are removed from the diet.

Cerebral Allergies and the Vitamin Dependencies (B-3 and B-6): The Adrenochrome Hypothesis of Schizophrenia[13,14,15,16]

The causal factors can lead to schizophrenia, but in each case there must be a final common pathway that accounts for the perceptual changes and thought disorder. It is my hypothesis that the adrenochrome reaction is the common end pathway. Thus, a cerebral allergy, or any of the other causes, will initiate the adrenochrome reaction.

The use of megadoses of vitamin B-3 and vitamin C was not serendipitous. It arose out of the adrenochrome hypothesis that my two colleagues and I first published in 1954. The hypothesis can be expressed with the following equations.

(1) noradrenalin + methyl group $\longrightarrow$ adrenalin
(2) adrenalin + oxygen $\longrightarrow$ adrenochrome

Earlier, Osmond and Smythies[17] had suggested that a substance related to adrenalin with the psychological properties of mescalin, one of the hallucinogenic drugs, might be present in the schizophrenic's body. This was the first transmethylation hypothesis in psychiatry. Transmethylation is a reaction that transfers a methyl group from one substance to another. Equation 1 is an example of a transmethylation reaction.

Later we centered our investigation on adrenochrome.

This is the first oxidation derivative of adrenalin. Equation 2 is an oxidation reaction easily seen when a pure solution of adrenalin is exposed to air and turns pink, then later becomes more discolored and turns gray or black. The early research that I directed in Saskatchewan arose out of this very useful observation. We hypothesized that schizophrenia is one of the oxidation-reduction diseases, that is, it results from excessive free radical formation (hyperoxidation) and too little antioxidant concentration. Therefore, treatment should try to decrease the hyperoxidation and increase the concentration of antioxidants. We have tested ascorbic acid but there have been few tests of the other antioxidants such as vitamin E, the carotenoids, glutathione, uric acid, and selenium.

With a substantial, six-year Rockefeller Foundation grant to pursue these views and to expand our research in 1954, we showed that adrenochrome is an hallucinogen that could be made in the body and proved our hypothesis, although our work was ignored for many years. Now we not only know that it is present in the body but we have methods by which it can be accurately measured. The adrenochrome hypothesis has been highlighted in a series of excellent reports by John Smythies.[18,19,20,21,22]

Schizophrenia is a very complex biochemical disorder involving tryptophan, vitamin B-3, vitamin B-6, ascorbic acid, folic acid, vitamin B-12, EFAs, zinc, and chemicals made in the body such as adrenalin and other catecholamines, serotonin, prostaglandins, and many others. But I think that adrenochrome and similar substances will play major roles in the end point of the disease, at the synaptic levels in the brain.

The adrenochrome hypothesis accounts for a large number of the physical and psychological findings in schizophrenic patients. We described these in our book, *The Hallucinogens*.[23] As an interesting aside, the fact that schizophrenia still exists in all human populations proves that it is a genetic -morphism. This means that while there is no advantage in being sick with schizophrenia, there is some advantage conferred by carrying the genes: having enough of them without becoming sick. First-order relatives are a case in point: in the

Darwinian sense of being biologically superior, they are reproductively successful. Schizophrenics themselves tend to be physically superior to nonschizophrenics[24] and appear more youthful (even in old age); their hair does not turn gray as early as the normal population's would; they have higher tolerance to pain; they do not have as high an incidence of arthritis or cancer; and they are more resistant to bacterial infections. They also seem to be more creative, a psychological trait due perhaps to their inner experiences with perceptual changes.

We hoped we could treat schizophrenics successfully by slowing down the transformation process from adrenalin to adrenochrome. We thought that we could decrease the formation of adrenalin from noradrenalin, a methyl acceptor, by using large doses of another methyl acceptor, vitamin B-3. By the addition of a methyl group, noradrenalin becomes adrenalin. Decreasing the amount of adrenalin would therefore decrease the amount of adrenochrome. We therefore decided to give our patients large doses of this vitamin, hoping it would soak up the methyl groups and thus stop the excessive formation of adrenalin. We also knew that pellagra was one of the schizophrenic-like conditions and in its early stages often could not be differentiated from schizophrenia. Vitamin B-3 was safe, with a huge LD^{50} in animals, about 4 grams per kilogram body weight. For a 70-kilogram person this would be over one-half pound of vitamin per day.

This hypothesis also pointed toward ascorbic acid as another very useful substance. Ascorbic acid is a water-soluble reducing agent, the body's best water-soluble antioxidant. It is more difficult for the adrenalin to be oxidized into adrenochrome in the presence of ascorbic acid. We realized that we would need to use very large doses if we were going to use this reaction in the body. As far as I can tell, this is one of the first uses of the antioxidant series of compounds such as vitamin E, selenium, coenzyme Q10, and glutathione that are so commonly used today. What we did not know in 1954 was that the presence of scurvy was used in the differential diagnosis in psychotic patients around the turn of the twentieth century because it produced a schizophrenic-like syndrome. In summary, vitamin B-3 could decrease the formation of adrenalin, and vitamin C would make it more difficult for the body to oxidize the adrenalin to adrenochrome.

The first time I used megadoses of vitamin C in the early 1950s, I saw a remarkable therapeutic response. A middle-aged woman with breast cancer was admitted to our psychiatric ward. The operative site of her mastectomy had become infected, was suppurating, and would not heal. At the same time, she became psychotic. Her psychiatric diagnosis was schizophrenia and her psychiatrist ordered electroconvulsive therapy (ECT) to commence the following week. (This was before the tranquilizer drugs had been introduced and ECT was the only treatment available.) For reasons I now do not remember, I decided to give her a megadose of vitamin C, perhaps 3 grams each day, and asked her psychiatrist whether he would delay the ECT for a few weeks so that I could try out the vitamin C. He agreed that he would delay giving her ECT for a few days. I therefore ordered that she be given 1 gram of vitamin C every hour, day and night. If she slept, the vitamin C was held, and when she awakened, what she had not taken was given to her. From Saturday morning to the following Monday morning she was given 45 grams. When her psychiatrist came to give her the ECT, he found her mentally normal and she was discharged to her home one week later without ECT. To my amazement, the ulcerated mass on her chest had begun to heal with fresh granulation tissue. Although she died six months later from her cancer, she had remained mentally normal. I was not a breast cancer researcher and did not follow that observation until many years later, but I was impressed with the vitamin's effect on her psychosis and after that used vitamin C on as many patients as possible.

The adrenochrome hypothesis describes the final common pathway for this disease, but schizophrenia may be triggered by a number of conditions. Probably every factor I have listed earlier as causing the syndrome will activate the adrenochrome pathway. For this reason, the best treatment must eliminate the causal factors and at the same time neutralize the adrenochrome pathways. Our book, *The Hallucinogens*,[23] provides a complete description of the adrenochrome hypothesis and how it accounts for most of the clinical phenomena found in schizophrenia.

THE THERAPEUTIC REGIMEN[25,26,27,28,29]

The therapeutic regimen includes several nutrients and drugs that must be added to the basic nutritional recommendations given to a patient. This regimen is a simple one that any physician can offer, even a practitioner who does not have access to laboratories for some of the tests that are now available.

This regimen is not necessarily followed by all orthomolecular physicians; however, every orthomolecular physician will follow its underlying principles while using different combinations of nutrients and medications to achieve the desired responses.

HOW THE PHYSICIAN MAKES A PROBABLE DIAGNOSIS

Because the diagnosis is so important, the first step of the treatment is to determine the most probable diagnosis. I am interested in the history of the illness so I listen to the patients and to members of their families, guiding them with the right questions. I do not routinely ask about the psychodynamic factors usually sought by analysts and psychotherapists. After the history, I spend a lot of time assessing all the areas of the mental state including perceptual changes, thought disorder, mood changes, and behavioral changes—this is the most important aspect of the diagnosis since it determines what the treatment will be. I may use one of the two diagnostic perceptual tests I listed above. Once I am reasonably certain of the diagnosis, I advise the patient and family of it. If it is schizophrenia, I will tell them this is not a mental disorder but a biochemical disorder that expresses itself in mental symptoms. Schizophrenia is not caused by trauma, anxiety, or childhood factors, even though these may influence the disease. It is caused by unknown genetic factors as well as the other etiological factors described earlier that influence biochemistry and cause the body to generate toxins or chemicals which adversely react within and upon the brain. I outline my recommendations for a therapeutic regimen and estimate how much time it will take long before they are much improved or fully recovered. I send all results of such a consultation to the referring physician.

CEREBRAL ALLERGIES

Taking a complete nutritional history is a crucial part of the examination. I ask about food allergies and how they were expressed early in life, such as colic in infancy, frequent sore throats, frequent colds, enlarged adenoids and tonsils, rashes, flu, asthma, and so on. If the history suggests a food allergy is involved, I explore the patient's food preferences. The favorite foods are usually the ones that the patient is allergic to. If food allergies are suspected, I will suggest regimens such as elimination diets and rotation diets designed to elicit what these allergies are. An elimination diet lasts several weeks and omits the food or foods that may be responsible for the allergic reaction. If there is marked improvement at the end of this period, that food is reintroduced and if it causes a recurrence of symptoms, we can establish a diagnosis that shows food is a factor. In a rotation diet the same foods are not repeated each day. There are four-day, five-day, and seven-day diets. With the seven-day diet the same foods are eaten every seventh day. I find the four-day water fast, a special category of elimination diet since it eliminates all foods, to be very useful. Over a period of several years I fasted over 200 of my schizophrenic patients.

Some Memorable Case Histories Involving Cerebral Allergies
   The first three patients were the most memorable, because

the effect of removing the offending allergen was so striking. Two sisters came to see me in 1970, one a local resident in Saskatoon, the other from Toronto. The Toronto sister had been ill for three years and had a history of three psychiatric hospital admissions during that time period. She was very paranoid and suspicious that her husband was poisoning her and became so fearful she fled to her sister in Saskatoon to get away from her husband. The woman was clearly schizophrenic but I could not get her admitted to the local hospital at which I had privileges, so I suggested that she and her sister try a four-day water fast. I was familiar with the cerebral allergy concept by then but frankly did not know if such a fast would help the patient. I actually thought it most unlikely that she would respond and hoped I could buy some time until a hospital bed became available. Her sister promised to help. The patient was instructed to start the fast the next day by avoiding breakfast. She was to eat nothing for four days, but had to drink at least 8 glasses of water each day. The two women were given an outline of how to reintroduce foods one at a time into the patient's diet and they were to test four different foods each day. Every food item that did not produce any paranoid or other symptoms was to be added to the diet. She completed the fast and began to test the foods, but not one of them was an offender. She remained well. She had recovered by the fifth day, called her husband in Toronto and said something like, "Dear, I am so sorry I was so foolish. May I come home?" As she continued the process of testing foods she developed pain in one hip and took an aspirin tablet. Within hours she was very paranoid again. This woman's situation was a clearcut example of an aspirin allergy causing her schizophrenic syndrome. Then I discovered that she had suffered from hip pain for over two years and had been using aspirin the entire time, even when she was admitted to the psychiatric wards. Since I had advised that all medication not be taken during the fast, she had not taken the aspirin. A few days later, recovered, she flew back to her home in Toronto.

The second patient was a middle-aged man who had been depressed for at least four years. He had been treated for schizophrenia in a mental hospital for many months. His wife had left him because she could not tolerate his abnormal behavior. After discharge, he was being cared for by an aunt. I tried the four-day water fast with him and instructed him not to smoke or take any medications. I was actually looking for patients who wouldn't respond to this regimen! But, like the previous patient, his symptoms cleared up and he found no foods that triggered another depressive episode. He began to smoke again a week after completing his fast. His depression returned as soon as he did so. He quit smoking again and remained well. One month after treatment, he was able to return to work as a high school principal. The insurance company that had been paying him support sent a representative from Vancouver to Saskatoon to find out what I had done that had rehabilitated this man so quickly. The irony was that his brother was a tobacco company executive and had been supplying him with free cartons of cigarettes.

The third case was a catatonic young woman who was so rigid with tension that she could not walk. I first examined her in her home and promptly ordered an ambulance to take her to the hospital. However, she did not respond to my nutrient regimen. Since I was familiar by then with Dr. Allan Cott's visit to Moscow where he had observed the fasting treatment for chronic schizophrenic patients,[34] I asked my patient if she would try the Russian protocol. She agreed. Amazingly, she was normal after the fifth day. But as I was not yet aware of the allergy concept, I continued the fast to its conclusion and since she was still well at that point, I began to reintroduce foods. Within a few days she again became sick. I could not fast her again right away because she had lost so much weight. I kept her in the hospital until she had regained enough weight and then fasted her, but this time only for five days. She again recovered. I then found out she was allergic to all meats. When she avoided meat she was normal and stayed normal. Her situation illustrates a severe allergic reaction to animal protein.

These three examples were so striking that I began to fast

those patients who had not recovered or who responded only partially. Approximately 200 patients were asked to do the fast. Only ten percent were fasted in the hospital. Out of the total group, about 60 percent were allergic to foods and when these foods were eliminated, they improved or became normal. As a result, I came to believe that cerebral allergy plays a major role in the etiology of the schizophrenic syndrome. I have become more skillful at determining the potential food allergies over the past twenty years, so I have fasted very few patients during that time period. The elimination diets are just as effective in discovering the offending substances and are easier for the patients to handle. But even when there are no allergies I advise the elimination of all junk food, especially those that contain added sugars. That step will effectively cleanse most modern diets by about 90 percent. Foods containing added sugars invariably contain other additives.

VITAMINS

VITAMIN B-3

Vitamin B-3 (the term brought back into the literature by Bill W., cofounder of Alcoholics Anonymous) refers to nicotinic acid and nicotinamide, more often called niacin and niacinamide in medical literature.[35] Both are precursors to nicotinamide adenine dinucleotide (NAD), the active coenzyme in the body, and share similar properties. However, they also differ. Niacin is a vasodilator: It lowers triglycerides and total cholesterol, and elevates high density lipoprotein cholesterol. Niacinamide has no effect on the lipid profile.

Safety and Side Effects

Although both forms are safe,[36] each has side effects. Too high a dose of niacinamide can cause nausea, often resulting in vomiting. The dose should be decreased whenever there is nausea. Allergic reactions are possible but unpredictable.

The most common and least dangerous side effect with niacin is the vasodilatation or flushing accompanied by a sensation of itching and heat because niacin opens the capillaries in the skin and increases blood flow. The flush may last anywhere from several minutes to several hours; it usually starts in the forehead and travels down the body. Rarely, it envelops the whole body. The most intense flush can be expected the first time it is taken; subsequently, it fades until it is barely noticeable. Vitamin use must be discontinued if the flush remains intolerable.

Flush intensity depends upon the rate of niacin absorption into the blood. If it is injected intravenously, the flush will be most intense. Most people take it by mouth, however. Dissolving it in hot tea and drinking the mixture on an empty stomach will also produce an intense flush. You can reduce the intensity of the flush by having food in your stomach and by drinking a cold drink. Other flush reduction strategies are to take aspirin a few days before starting niacin therapy or to take an antihistamine such as Periactin half an hour before ingestion of niacin.

One form of niacin is a slow-releasing formulation; though flush is reduced or nonexistent, very few serious liver complications have occurred with use of this product, but the source of the side effect is unknown. The second form—inositol niacinate (hexaniacin inositol)—is an ester of inositol and niacin. It is flush-free, more easily tolerated, and just as effective as the flush-producing varieties. It has not been reported to cause any liver complications, but is a more expensive product.

Schizophrenics generally do not flush much, not nearly as much as other patients. Often they do not flush at all until they have started to recover. This is now the basis for a diagnostic test developed by Horrobin.[44] As with an overdose of niacinamide, nausea leading to vomiting is a side effect of niacin use if the dose is too high. This reaction may be used as a way of determining the optimum dose—that is, one increases the dose until there is some nausea and then decreases it to just below that level to get the maximum effective dosage for that patient.

A more serious and much rarer side effect is an obstructive type of jaundice, which clears when the niacin is discontinued. The usual liver function tests are misleading because they may read high when niacin is taken, suggesting there is a liver problem when, in fact, there is none. Therefore niacin should not be taken for five days before these liver tests are run. They will then be normal. It is probably an artifact. If tests are normal, liver damage did not exist; if damage is present, the results would not show normal values so quickly. However, niacin should be discontinued immediately at the first sign of jaundice. It is possible that someone who had jaundice as a side effect with one course of niacin therapy can try it again with no recurrence. I have not seen any cases of jaundice for at least ten years. If a patient has high cholesterol or heart disease, niacin therapy is indicated and may increase their life span.

Dosages

The usual therapeutic dose for schizophrenics is between 3 and 6 grams daily in three divided doses, after meals. I usually start with 3 grams and will increase it after several months if the response is too slow. The dosage range is enormous. I have had patients on 30 grams daily with no discomfort and one subject, a young girl with schizophrenia, increased the dose on her own until she was taking 60 grams daily. At that level, the voices she had been constantly hearing vanished. Later, she was able to maintain herself on 3 grams. Patients should take niacin in these large doses only under medical supervision. It is not possible to go to such high dosages with niacinamide because it causes nausea at lower doses than does niacin. The most frequent dose range is 3 to 4.5 grams daily. After patients have become well, the dose may be decreased to a lower maintenance level. I think that most of my patients do this anyway and will often find out how much they need to take to stay well.

Duration of Treatment

There is a direct relationship between the duration of the disease and the amount of time needed to achieve recovery, and therapists must have enough patience to stay with their patients until they do recover. Treatment with vitamin B-3, and with the other components of the program, continues until the patient is well, and should then carry on until there is reason to believe that no relapse will occur if the program is discontinued. Recovery may take many years if the patient has been sick for many years. Unfortunately, not everyone will get well, but most will.

VITAMIN B-6 (PYRIDOXINE)

When I was Director of Psychiatric Research in Saskatchewan between 1960 and 1967, we found that when the urine of early schizophrenic patients was tested, up to 75 percent of them had a mauve staining area on the paper chromatogram containing kryptopyrrole. Dr. C. C. Pfeiffer and his research group showed that this substance bound both zinc and vitamin B-6, producing a double deficiency. The treatment for this condition was to supply both of these nutrients. The detection of this condition has been described by Pfeiffer.[37]

Pyridoxine is safe when used in the usual dose ranges. At doses greater than 2,000 milligrams daily, and in the absence of other vitamins, it can cause a peripheral neuropathy which clears when the vitamin is discontinued. I have seen no side effects for daily doses under 1,000 milligrams. If given to children B-6 should be combined with magnesium, since it tends to increase their activity levels when used alone. I usually use it in combination with vitamin B-3.

VITAMIN C

I use 3 grams of vitamin C daily but may go higher if there is a special need to do so, though schizophrenic patients don't usually require such high doses. The optimum levels are those just below the laxative level. This effect has been called a toxic reaction, but technically it is not, because it simply arises from the inability of the patient to absorb it all and it therefore draws fluid into the bowel. Vitamin C is extraordinarily safe. Contrary to the fiction propagated by some physicians, it does not cause kidney stones, pernicious anemia, or sterility, nor does it destroy the blood. Furthermore, it has great value in alleviating the symptoms of the common cold.[38]

FOLIC ACID AND VITAMIN B-12

More research should be done about the roles of folic acid and vitamin B-12 in the treatment of schizophrenics. DeLiz[39] used it in combination with niacin. Dr. L. Kotkas treats many schizophrenic patients with large doses of folic acid and B-12. These vitamins and vitamin B-3 are involved in transmethylation reactions, which are probably very important in schizophrenia, but B-12 also improves the flow of red blood cells through the capillaries (Simpson[40,41]). Blood flow through the frontal lobes of the brains of schizophrenic patients tends to be low. Any therapeutic measure which will improve this blood flow ought to be helpful. Large-scale trials are warranted.

ESSENTIAL FATTY ACIDS (EFA)

Both classes of EFAs are important. In modern diets there is more apt to be a deficiency of omega-3 EFA compared to omega-6 EFAs. Linoleic acid is the precursor to the omega-6 series. However, many patients experienced a partial block in its conversion to the next members of the chain. Evening primrose oil and other oils contain gamma linolenic acid, which is converted into dihomogammalinolenic acid, which, in turn, is the precursor to prostaglandins, series 1 and 2. Horrobin[42,43,44,45] suggests that the EFAs and the prostaglandins are involved in the biochemical pathology of schizophrenia. Rudin[46] found flaxseed oil therapeutic for schizophrenic patients. He describes two types of pellagra (one of the schizophrenic syndromes). The best known is caused by the deficiency of vitamin B-3. This is needed in the conversion of EFAs to prostaglandins. But if there is a deficiency of EFAs—even with adequate amounts of vitamin B-3—there will still be a deficiency of prostaglandins. He calls the first the "vitamin deficiency" type and the second the "EFA deficiency" type.[47,48] Thus, in treating schizophrenia, one must take into account the provision of all of the essential nutrients, including the EFAs.

MINERALS

ZINC AND COPPER

Kryptopyrrole was found in the majority of schizophrenic patients in Saskatchewan.[49,50] After it was identified, Carl Pfeiffer—formerly Director of Research at the Brain Bio Center near Princeton, New Jersey, a facility that no longer exists—studied it intensively, named it pyroluria, discovered that it bound both pyridoxine and zinc, thus causing a double deficiency, and described it clinically. He considered that pyroluria characterized one of the three main variants of schizophrenia, the other two being the high histamine and the low histamine groups. This work drew attention to the role of zinc and copper since these minerals have an inverse relationship in the body. To lower copper one can increase zinc levels. The book, *Mental and Elemental Nutrients*, contains the first detailed description of the role played by zinc and copper in schizophrenia.

Pfeiffer[51,52] emphasized the copper as a negative factor and zinc as a positive factor. In the large series of patients tested in his laboratory, very few patients had too little copper—most had too much. He prepared a liquid solution containing 10 percent zinc sulfate and 0.5 percent manganese chloride and gave patients up to ten or more drops per day of this preparation. I have found this to be very helpful in treating patients with tardive dyskinesia, and I usually use one per day of the common zinc tablets containing 50 milligrams of zinc.

SELENIUM

Selenium is a good antioxidant with antidepressant properties, so it should be a valuable adjunct for treating schizophrenia.[53] Foster[54] conducted a massive survey of the relationship of various diseases to the composition of the soils for minerals. He found that the prevalence of schizophrenia is increased where fodder crops are selenium deficient. The correlation coefficient was 0.58, a very high association for natural phenomena. The hypothesis that there is a relation between low selenium levels and increased incidence of schizophrenia is further supported by more recent data.[55] He also found a negative correlation between mercury levels and schizophrenia. Selenium is an antidote to mercury. Dietary deficiency of selenium increases the difficulty in making prostaglandins in the body. The antioxidant glutathione peroxidase (selenoenzyme) contains selenium. These findings suggest that selenium ought to be used in the treatment of schizophrenia. I use 200 to 600 micrograms daily.

MANGANESE

Tardive dyskinesia is a neuromuscular reaction similar to Parkinson's disease. It causes various tremors and random movements and can affect any group of muscles. It may be irreversible and can be very debilitating. The most serious side effect of the tranquilizers was tardive dyskinesia until clozapine came along with an even more serious side effect: death. Thus, if clozapine is used, extraordinary precautions, including blood counts every two weeks, must be taken to safeguard the patient's life. As new drugs were developed, this neuromuscular toxic side effect just described was minimized to some degree. However, the drug companies have ignored the best solution of all—to provide manganese. If each tablet of tranquilizer were to contain microgram amounts of manganese it is likely this condition would not develop. Kunin[56] showed that giving manganese would remove tardive dyskinesia in most patients, and that using manganese in combination with niacin worked even better. I have confirmed his observation and routinely add manganese to the regimen when I see a patient upon intake who is already suffering from tardive dyskinesia. I have rarely seen this condition in patients I have treated from the onset of their disease, but if and when such symptoms appeared, manganese therapy promptly removed them. I use 30 milligrams of the chelated manganese or Carl Pfeiffer's preparation—that is, 5 to 10 drops daily of a solution containing 10 percent zinc sulfate and 0.5 percent manganese chloride. Patients treated by orthomolecular methods do not get tardive dyskinesia.

MEDICATION

TRANQUILIZERS

The most commonly used drugs are the tranquilizers, first discovered around 1950 and introduced to North America in 1955, and the antidepressants, an offshoot of the tranquilizers discovered about 1956 and rapidly introduced to North America. We began our vitamin B-3 and vitamin C studies before these drugs had been discovered. Chlorpromazine (thorazine in the U.S.) came from France, where it was first used. It was rejected by most academics and especially by the National Institute of Mental Health (NIMH), which at that time was under the thumb of psychoanalysts. The drug was more readily accepted by psychiatrists working in mental hospitals after they saw how quickly and effectively it controlled a patient's psychotic behavior.

It took a combination of immense and intense pressure from a large number of senators and congressmen led by Mary Lasker before NIMH shifted its position about the tranquilizers. Mrs. Lasker was influential in Washington, and the Lasker award was sought by many prominent scientists. It took her determination and the help of many others to achieve a change in NIMH. The drug companies saw the huge potential in these drugs and soon had persuaded almost all psychiatrists that tranquilizers were the answer to the treatment of schizophrenia. It is true that these drugs are very effective, and newer ones have been developed over the years. The problem with the all the drugs used was that they were only partially effective and had many undesirable side effects, such as dry mouth and tardive dyskinesia.

The Holy Grail is a tranquilizer which will cure the patients and have no side effects. In fact we already have it: the orthomolecular regimen. Unfortunately, it has not been recognized and does not have multi-billion-dollar drug companies to promote it. Though the newer drugs have fewer troublesome side effects than their predecessors, none are more effective than orthomolecular regimens in restoring the patients to health.

Tranquilizers and Recovery: A Catch-22
Reliance on tranquilizers alone creates a major dilemma for both the patients and the psychiatrists. The problem becomes obvious as soon as one recognizes three facts.

1. Tranquilizers are helpful in reducing the intensity of the psychotic symptomatology (obvious to anyone who has ever used these compounds), but they do not remove them.
2. Tranquilizers make normal people sick (obvious to anyone who has taken them in error, or to the Russians who, committed to hospitals as dissidents, were placed on tranquilizers such as thorazine, and were made psychotic this way). These drugs produced catatonic reactions in animals, one of the early tests of drug efficacy.
3. Schizophrenia is a chronic disease. Once established it has a momentum of its own and runs on and on until it is interrupted by some therapeutic measure.

Spontaneous recovery from schizophrenia is rare. Partial recovery is more typical—many of these patients no longer complain of visual or auditory hallucinations but will suffer from chronic depression or anxiety. In many cases, the thought disorder becomes manifest only under severe stress, and for many only under the influence of alcohol. I have seen many alcoholic patients who are very paranoid when drunk but do not display these symptoms when sober. Estimates of recovery don't include the group of partially improved patients; instead, they are included in the "recovered" group for statistical analysis so it looks as if the rate of recovery is 33 percent. My opinion is that the true figure is probably closer to 10 percent and is based on the large number of patients I have seen who have never had to go back to mental hospitals but who remained ill.

The problem with tranquilizer use is this. The drugs start the process of recovery by reducing the intensity and frequency of symptoms and signs. But it becomes a Catch-22: As the patient becomes more clinically and biochemically "normal," that person begins to react more and more as if she or he were normal, which means they become psychotic from the drug. We are considering two different psychoses—the initial schizophrenic psychosis described earlier, and the tranquilizer-induced or iatrogenic psychosis characterized by both physical and psychological symptoms. Physical side effects range from mild to severe, with the shaking and tremors and grotesque involuntary muscular movements of tardive dyskinesia being the most severe. Interest in sex may wane; males may also become impotent and refuse to remain on the drugs.

Psychologically, side effects may include perceptual changes, but they tend to be less intense than if the patient were not medicated at all. The same is true of thought disorder—although it is not as troublesome, there is increased difficulty in concentration, memory problems occur, and the patients become increasingly preoccupied with themselves. Inertia, flat affect, and an inability to feel sorrow or happiness are all side effects of tranquilizer use. Many of these tranquilized patients lose the qualities that make men and women spontaneous, responsive, interested, and interesting. In most cases, they cannot work in any responsible positions. I personally would not allow a surgeon on 6 milligrams of resperidal to operate on me, nor would I want my bus driver to be on 50 milligrams of Haldol.

So, this is the dilemma. How can we transform the original psychosis back into the normal state without inducing the tranquilizer psychosis? Psychiatrists attempt to deal with this problem by decreasing the doses and eventually taking their patients off the offending drug or by placing them on a new drug. But since the disease process is still active, when the drug dose is reduced too far, the original schizophrenia-induced psychosis returns. Patients deal with this problem by refusing to take the medication, preferring to be ill with their original psychosis rather than having to suffer the ravages of the iatrogenic psychosis. Thus, patients tend to flip back and forth between these two psychoses. Orthomolecular psychiatry gives them a third and appropriate choice—to become well.

The Partnership of Tranquilizer Therapy and Orthomolecular Regimens

Tranquilizers work very quickly. This makes them valuable to psychiatrists who want to see rapid control of a disease state. But tranquilizers do not allow the patient to recover. On the other hand, nutrients work very slowly. They often need many months to become optimally effective. However, they never make anyone psychotic. By combining the two types of regimens using drugs and nutrients, it is possible to take advantage of the rapid effect of the drugs. When the nutrients have become effective, the amount of drugs needed to manage the psychoses can be gradually reduced. The healthier the person is, the less the drug will be needed. In most cases, patients will no longer need any drugs and will remain well on the nutrients alone. This resolves the dilemma of side effects and compliance with therapy. Some patients need very low doses of drugs, so low that there are no side effects. Many patients learn how to use the tranquilizers as needed, much as one would take an aspirin for headaches.

ANTIDEPRESSANTS AND THE ORTHOMOLECULAR REGIMEN

Antidepressants should be used when depression is a major component of the schizophrenia. I started using clomipramine many years ago for my paranoid patients who were not deeply depressed. It occurred to me that I had never seen a cheerful paranoid person. There seems to be a very strong correlation between being paranoid and being depressed. This suggested that if I could lift the mood of these paranoid patients, it would become easier to dispel their paranoid ideas. Furthermore, clomipramine was also still the best antidepressant for the obsessive compulsive conditions. Paranoid ideas often have this same type of obsessive characteristics. To test my theory, I added clomipramine to the treatment regimen of a chronic schizophrenic who had been ill since he was thirteen and who had remained paranoid throughout his therapy. For example, he was afraid to leave the house because he "knew" that the children half a block away were talking about him. After three months on clomipramine, his paranoid ideas had receded and, after several years on that antidepressant, were almost gone. Eventually, I was able to take him off the clomipramine and he remained much improved. I have used this approach many times over the years, and in most cases it works well.

OTHER MEDICATION AND THE ORTHOMOLECULAR REGIMEN

Drugs such as lithium, the benzodiazepines, anticonvulsants and so on, are used for the same conditions in the same ways as they would be by any traditional psychiatrist. The orthomolecular program is compatible with all medications. Over the course of treatment, the amount of drug needed in combination with the orthomolecular program is very much lower than it is when drugs alone are used. This is one of the reasons why tardive dyskinesia is not seen as a side effect when orthomolecular treatment is used in conjunction with other medications.

I have treated several patients with tardive dyskinesia (TD). I start them on the regimen and add manganese. Kunin showed that the combination of manganese and vitamin B-3 was very effective in preventing and treating TD.

A survey by Dr. David Hawkins,[57] one of the pioneers in this field, showed that in over 58,000 patients treated by orthomolecular doctors there were no cases of TD. This in itself is an adequate reason for the nutrients to be used.

PATIENTS ALREADY ON MEDICATION

The following case history illustrates my treatment program. Every patient is, of course, unique, and will need an approach that is best suited to that person. But this patient's treatment history is a model on which the orthomolecular treatment can be based. (I assume that most readers of this discussion will not have access to the more sophisticated modern tests for allergies, for blood levels of amino acids and vitamins, etc. A survey of these tests is available from Kunin,[58] whose book describes, references, and codes over fifty procedures.)

Michael, born in 1927, was brought to my office by his wife[A] and brother in June 1993. He was obese (250 pounds at 5 foot 11 inches), confused, and appeared retarded. He showed no emotional reaction and answered questions briefly. I had to depend on his relatives to give me his history. He had not worked for ten years.

He married at age twenty-seven and shortly after that was treated in a psychiatric ward for his first mental breakdown. At age forty-six he suffered another breakdown, and he was admitted again at age fifty-nine and improved after three weeks on medication. However, he had been deteriorating steadily during the year before I saw him and had become so confused he could not drive. During the course of his illness he had about five series of electroconvulsive therapy during at least five hospitalizations.

He displayed perceptual and thought disorder characteristic of the schizophrenic syndrome. He heard voices, believed that people were staring at him, was very paranoid, and believed people were plotting against him. He had often complained to his wife about the telephone being bugged. His memory and concentration were very poor, and he was confused. At times he was agitated and excited, but he never had manic-depressive mood swings. He was medicated daily with 800 milligrams of chlorpromazine, 900 milligrams of lithium, and 32 milligrams of perphenazine. He needed to take a drug to protect him against the side effects of these drugs. These are very high doses, so high I have seldom had to use these levels in forty-five years of psychiatry.

He met my diagnostic criteria for schizophrenia. I discussed this with him and his family, and told him that schizophrenia[B] was a biochemical disorder and that it was best treated by the use of the right nutrients in combination with the drugs he was then taking.[C] Then I advised him to change to a sugar-free diet, adding 1 gram each of niacin and ascorbic acid[D] after each meal. The vitamin C was added to reduce the bodily stress of the enormous drug doses. I told him I wanted him to avoid sweets, except for fruit, in order to remove most of the additives from his diet and to help him lose weight. There was no evidence he suffered from food allergies.

One month[E] later, he was a little better. His family had decreased his chlorpromazine (CPZ) ("thorazine" in the U.S.) to 700 milligrams daily. By the end of that year he had lost thirteen pounds, was on 300 milligrams of CPZ, and 16 milligrams of perphenazine. His family members were pleased with his progress as they saw his pre-illness personality reemerging.

One month later, he developed severe chills, fever, confusion, and a bladder infection, and was nearly comatose. He was admitted to hospital where the doctor in charge would not permit him to take vitamins. Each day in the hospital, off his vitamins, he deteriorated more and more, and was started on resperidal.[F] After discharge, his family stopped the new drug and restarted my regimen.[G] He was now on 600 milligrams lithium, 16 milligrams perphenazine, 200 milligrams CPZ. On March 22, 1994, I increased his niacin to 2 grams after each meal.[H] His mood was good. By the end of April, he weighed 223 pounds and was walking a lot more. The voices were receding and he was much less paranoid. I decreased his CPZ to 150 milligrams. On June 9, I added 1,200 milligrams (international units) of vitamin E and decreased the CPZ to 100 milligrams.[I] But a month later I had to increase it to 125 as he developed nausea.[J] He had now gone for entire days without hearing any voices. I added 5 milligrams of folic acid three times each day.[K]

By October 1994, he was normal. By December 1994 his CPZ dose was decreased to 50 milligrams; his weight had dropped to 217 pounds. He continued to improve and by June 1995, the voices were gone, his memory was much better, and he was off all medication. When he had difficulty sleeping in September 1995, I added 2 grams of tryptophan to be taken on an empty stomach before bed. Early in 1996, he would take 50 milligrams of CPZ occasionally. In July 1997 he was still normal. The last time I saw him he was alert, relaxed, at ease, spoke easily, and joked with his wife. We discussed his painting when I discovered he was an artist. I thought he was normal as did his wife; he had no complaints and felt well.

He fulfilled my criteria for recovery: he was symptom free and got on well with his family and with the community. I expected he would be back at his artist profession. He had reached my therapeutic objective: to get him off drugs, cured of his tranquilizer psychosis, and cured of his schizophrenia. The odds are very good that he will not relapse as long as he remains on his orthomolecular program. If relapse does occur, he might need some revision of his treatment. He will do well unless he falls into the hands of a psychiatrist who does not believe the nutrient program helped him, and insists he again be put on the tranquilizers from which he had suffered so much for so many years.

After the patients recover, I advise them to stay on the orthomolecular program for at least five years, or better still, for the rest of their lives. It leads to a dramatic improvement in the quality of life and probably an increase in life span as well.[59] Notes on this patient's treatment:

A. I find it very helpful to have the family in my office during the interview, with the patient's permission. A lot of time is saved in gathering the information needed to make the diagnosis. It also helps when the family hears the discussion and knows what the treatment will be. Although most psychiatrists no longer blame the family for the illness of a relative, it can still occur. It is important to remove any guilt the family may have derived from previous outmoded, harmful explanations.

B. Although my patient was clearly schizophrenic, he also showed all the features of the tranquilizer psychosis I discussed earlier. The problem was how to get him off the medication that was destroying him without causing a relapse into his schizophrenic state. I did not have to talk to his family about the tranquilizer psychosis. They had been aware of this for a long time. Patience is a very important factor in achieving a positive treatment outcome. If the drugs are withdrawn too rapidly, there is bound to be a marked reaction and a precipitous return to the original schizophrenic state, as the disease is still burning brightly in the body and the vitamin program has not had enough time to become fully operative. If a therapist does not have the patience to work for years with such a patient, it is a disservice to the patient to undertake the treatment.

C. The patient's obesity was caused by the excessively high intake of drugs and his resultant inactivity. It is important that a therapist do everything possible to restore the patient's self-confidence; helping them regain their earlier physical state is a good place to begin, so if they are too fat or too thin, this must be dealt with.

D. I prefer niacin for middle-aged men and women who may also have blood circulation problems in addition to their schizophrenia. Usually they can tolerate the initial flush without much discomfort.[60] Schizophrenic patients generally do not flush as much as nonschizophrenic patients. Dr. D. Horrobin[61,62,63] has developed a diagnostic test based upon this finding. He applies an adhesive strip containing four different concentrations of niacin. After five minutes, the strip is removed. He found that most patients with schizophrenia do not have any erythema, the areas under the strip do not turn red, whereas most other people do show the reddening reaction. There is very little overlap. This test will soon be available commercially. If the vasodilatation could cause embarrassment to the patients, or if they are younger, they may prefer to take niacinamide. Both are probably equally effective, but the advantage with niacin is that one can prescribe much higher dosage without getting the patient into the upper dosage limit marked by nausea. Often, schizophrenic patients do not flush at all at the beginning. Some have started flushing only after months or years of treatment and this physical reaction is accompanied by a sudden major clinical improvement.

E. If the patient is very psychotic or the family very disturbed I will agree to see them again in a week or two. However, in most cases patients already controlled by drugs do not have to be seen more frequently than every month. As they get better, the interval between visits is increased. When they are well, they no longer need to see me, but they know they can call me at any time to renew the therapeutic relationship.

F. Being denied access to their vitamins is a common problem for my patients who have to be admitted to a hospital. Doctors are so ignorant of the value of vitamins that they either fear using them or think them valueless. This attitude is declining as families and patients are become more forceful in demanding to be allowed to continue the vitamin program. A few of my patients have been so demanding that the hospital relented and allowed them to remain on the regimen. One of my patients, a young male, took vitamins the whole time he was in the hospital. The staff did not know this. He walked about in big boots with the tops unlaced; all his vitamins were hidden in his boots and he told me about this after discharge. He recovered. When patients are taken off the program they tend to deteriorate, and often after discharge I will have to start the orthomolecular program all over again. This is a pity; one day I hope that it will be considered unethical or even malpractice to force a patient to discontinue a vitamin regimen while an inpatient.

G. It is obvious that the patient and his family had no

trust nor respect for the doctors who were treating him in the hospital. They liked and trusted me and resented the attempts of the hospital doctors to interfere with my treatment. Having seen the effect of using drugs alone, they wanted no more of them.

H. I often double the dose of niacin if I want to accelerate the recovery. The increased niacin would make it easier to get off the drugs.

I. I have regretted not having run a therapeutic trial with vitamin C alone, one of the body's more effective water soluble antioxidants. Since schizophrenia is one of the free radical diseases, it makes sense to also treat schizophrenics with vitamin E, which of course has many other beneficial properties.

J. One way of determining the optimum dose of any drug is to either increase or decrease it. Symptoms will reappear if the dose is decreased too quickly and then the dose must be adjusted upward.

K. Folic acid participates in transmethylation reactions as does nicotinic acid. I find that adding folic acid improves its efficacy, at least in the treatment of atrial fibrillation, and I assume it will be equally helpful for schizophrenia. It has no side effects. It is available with prescription as 5-milligram tablets.

PATIENTS WHO ARE NOT ON MEDICATION

Most of the patients I see have already been diagnosed and started on treatment by other psychiatrists. They are referred to me only because they have not responded to the program they were advised to follow. But I do see a few who are becoming ill and who have not been treated. In those cases, I follow the same principles using the same nutritional and nutrient approach, but I may not use any medication. If they are very depressed I will use the antidepressants. If they are too anxious and restless, I will use the other drugs in combination. But almost every patient needs only small doses of the tranquilizers and the antidepressants until recovery, when they no longer need them.

ACUTE PATIENTS

"Acute" refers to the class of patients who are sick for the first time or who have recovered from an episode and have relapsed. We used this class of people in our six double-blind controlled experiments started in Saskatchewan in 1953 to 1960.

For our first double-blind experiment we randomized thirty patients into three groups: one was the placebo group, a second was given niacin (niacin cannot be blinded because of the flush), and the third took niacinamide, which does not cause any flush—this was our hidden control group. The clinical staff knew only that there would be two groups: placebo and niacin. They would therefore assume that all nonflushing patients were getting placebo, but in fact half of them were on niacinamide. We found out later that the vitamin groups yielded the same results. We found the usual 35 percent response over two years from the placebo group, and a 75 percent response from the vitamin groups.

The rest of the controlled experiments gave identical results.

Based on this early experience and upon my personal experience in treating over 4,000 patients since 1952, I can report with confidence that with this acute class of schizophrenics one should expect a 90 percent recovery rate if the therapeutic regimen is followed for at least two years under the supervision of a patient physician who is dedicated to getting the patient well.

Many years ago, a report appeared in the psychiatric press describing the outcome of treatment of about forty-two physicians who had become schizophrenic and were treated with drugs. The outcome was dismal. Only twelve were able to resume their practices, and of these, six were able to do so because their wives were nurses who ran their practices, with the schizophrenic doctors assuming responsibility for the patients' prescriptions. In sharp contrast, I know of seventeen teenage schizophrenic males who recovered on orthomolecular therapy. They went to college, became doctors, and today are practicing medicine and psychiatry. One of them, my patient, became the president of a major psychiatric organization in North America. Ironically, this very association attacked the work I was doing with vitamin therapy. They did not know that their president had failed to get well on placebo but did recover when given niacin. Of this small group, one is chairman of a large department in a medical school, one is a research psychiatrist, one heads a large clinic that he founded, and so on. Among the schizophrenic doctors I have treated, all recovered and became active in the orthomolecular field.

Every physician who has treated this class of patient with the regimen I have described has obtained identical therapeutic results. The specifics of these therapeutic results are described in many reports, most of which have been published in the *Journal of Orthomolecular Medicine.*[64,65,66, 67,68,69,70,71,72,73,74.]

CHRONIC SCHIZOPHRENIC PATIENTS

There are two classes of chronic patients: those permanently institutionalized and those who have managed to be cared for by resources other than institutions. Let us look at each category.

Those who have been permanently incarcerated in institutions. With the remarkable success of the deinstitutionalizing program in emptying the mental hospitals in North America, the majority of the patients have been dumped into nursing homes, run-down hotels, and, of course, the streets. About 35 to 50 percent of the homeless street people in the major cities are such chronic patients. Dr. T. P. Millar,[75] a Vancouver psychiatrist, concluded, "Maybe the back wards of our mental hospitals were bad but surely they were more humane than what is happening now. I suppose blaming hospital physicians for sending such sick persons out into the community dispose of the problem for the ignorant, both lay and professional. It sure doesn't do a thing for those demented souls freezing to death on our mean and uncaring streets."

I have had no experience in treating them. It would be impossible to do so unless they were in a hospital setting, since they need shelter and care, as well as good nutrition and support.

Chronic patients who have been sick continually or have had fluctuation in their illness, but have been cared for in their homes or have been able to find shelter somewhat better than one finds on the streets. With this latter group, the treating doctor must have a great deal of patience. I have often wondered why the first orthomolecular pioneers like Allan Cott, Harvey Ross, Moke Williams, Jack Ward, and many others, who were psychoanalysts by training and experience, were such good orthomolecular physicians. The reason became obvious later on. They were physicians who had been trained to be patient and caring. They were not accustomed to the in-and-out emergency-room mentality, in which hospitals are first aid stations designed to rapidly tranquilize patients and discharge them as soon as possible. Modern psychiatrists are accustomed to seeing very rapid responses to drugs; they do not have the patience to work gradually with their patients over the course of many years. Modern psychiatric wards are tranquilizer filling stations similar in function to gasoline filling stations. Patients are admitted for a refill and rapidly discharged, irrespective of their real mental conditions.

I have approximately 500 chronic patients under my care. They are seen from once per month to once every few years, depending on their need for program adjustment. I recently pulled out twenty-seven charts from my files and found that seventeen of them have reached a well status.[76] They had been sick, on average, for seven years before I saw them. They had failed to respond to any prior treatment including drugs or ECT, and they had remained on my program for ten years. In most, the major surge to recovery occurred at about seven years. Therefore, if treatment is discontinued too soon, the optimum therapeutic effect will not occur. One of my complaints about psychiatric hospitals is that on the rare occasion when my patients are admitted, the hospital promptly stops my whole program, places them on other medication, and takes away their vitamins. When they are discharged and return to me, I have to start them all over again.

The following history illustrates the slow pace of recovery in one patient and the happy final outcome. Lena came to see me in October 1988, with her father. When they walked into my office, my first impression was that she was either severely retarded or a chronic deteriorated schizophrenic. She was unable to tell me anything and sat looking to one side the whole time, afraid to look squarely at me. I obtained the first history from her father. During her sixth grade year in school, her parents were told that she was unable to learn. From then on, she went to special classes. About one month before she came to see me, she had fallen asleep in her chair and had spent the night there. Her parents awakened her. She accused them of trying to drown her and ran away. The police picked her up later on, called her parents, and took her home. Her father complained that she suffered from unusual blotchy skin and that her hands became very sweaty when she became excited.

The mental state examination revealed only that she was paranoid, believing people were saying nasty things about her. I concluded that she was a learning disordered adult, a condition present from childhood. I started her on 1 gram niacinamide after each meal, the same amount of vitamin C, 250 milligrams pyridoxine, and 50 milligrams zinc gluconate each day. Six months later, her skin was normal, she was less depressed, had more self-confidence, and found it easier to communicate. She was no longer paranoid.

During July 1988, she had to be admitted to the hospital. This time, she complained about hearing her parents' voices when they were not present. I rediagnosed her chronic schizophrenia. She was started on small doses of thioridazine and was discharged a few days later. She was admitted again in March 1990, after her mother had advised her to stop the tranquilizer. She was admitted for the last time in March 1990, for 7 days. She was discharged on the same vitamin program with 300 milligrams daily of thioridazine, the average dose for this tranquilizer. She no longer hallucinated her parents' voices.

By the end of 1990, I was able to reduce the drug to 100 milligrams daily. By the end of 1991, she was getting along well and working part-time. She had been free of the voices. The drug was decreased to 75 milligrams in April 1992. She was cheerful, working at the same job, getting along well with her fellow workers. She was on 25 milligrams of the drug plus the same vitamins in January 1993. She was less sleepy, more cheerful and communicative. I kept on reducing the drug, but at the end of 1994 had to increase it back to 50 milligrams. Early in 1996, the drug dose was down to 25 milligrams.

She came to see me in July 1996, very excited. She was free of all symptoms. She brought along her math test results and had scored 100 percent. She proudly showed me the certificate she had received for her scholastic performance. She was a better reader than the other patients in her class and was not afraid to read in front of them. She told me that she was very happy because her parents, who had not been getting along, had reconciled and were enjoying each other's company again for the first time in many years.

The woman I had seen eight years earlier no longer existed. She had been transformed from a sick-looking woman who had the appearance of a retarded person (as used to be portrayed in old textbooks of psychiatry) and who would answer my questions but would look off to the side, to a young woman who dressed well and spoke freely to me. She now enjoyed coming to the office and especially enjoyed saying hello to my secretary and getting a hug from her. She interacted more appropriately, spoke more spontaneously, and engaged me in conversation while looking at me. I wrote to the referring physician, "It is always a delight to see how much improvement Lena is showing as I continue to see her. Today she was feeling really good, was very cheerful, and was especially delighted because her parents, who apparently had not been talking to each other for years, are getting along very much better. I think she is doing great." Lena has met all four criteria for recovery, but does not earn enough to pay income tax. She has been sick so long that the handicap of those lost years has not yet been resolved. But she is learning more skills in a fine rehabilitative program. Without the vitamins, she would have remained the same dowdy, retarded-looking woman with no hope of ever getting any better. She remains well.

Another example is a paranoid schizophrenic man from Toronto who had been treated several times in different hospitals. His wife divorced him and his family disowned him. He drifted to Victoria and lived on our street for about three months. He was referred to me, and to my surprise, remained on the vitamin program. After his second visit, I advised him to remain in the care of his general practitioner who had referred him.

About eight years later, I met the patient in a supermarket when he came up and introduced himself to me. I found out he was looking for work. He had just graduated with a B.A. from the local university. He had reunited with his family, was well, and though unemployed, was taking part in community activities.

A third case was the woman who burned her house down in response to voices. She is now well and the proud owner of a company that employs about thirty people.

My experience with chronic patients has convinced me of the following things:

1. Chronic patients must be treated patiently and continuously, with adequate support.
2. A combination of medication and nutrient therapy offers the advantages of the rapid effect of the drugs and the slow curative effect of the nutrients. This permits a gradual reduction of medication until the dose is so low the drug no longer creates the tranquilizer psychosis.
3. Schizophrenia in children may take the form of a learning disorder so that normally intelligent persons appear to be retarded. Lifting the psychosis by means of orthomolecular therapy will remove the apparent learning difficulty.

About ten years ago in New Orleans we put on a one-and-a-half-day training session for physicians at a meeting of the Huxley Institute of Biosocial Research. During a break, I remarked to a psychiatrist taking the course that if he used the orthomolecular regimen for one year he would never give it up. I received a long letter about six months later. He started out by saying, "Dr. Hoffer: You told me that if I used the program for one year I would not give it up. You were wrong. I have used it only six months and I will never give it up." Then he told me he was working in a state clinic responsible for the care of 1,200 schizophrenic patients, and his job description meant supervising their injections of drugs. His work had become so frustrating and boring, because he had not seen any recoveries, that he was thinking of leaving his practice. But his world changed after he started the orthomolecular program. He became very interested and was eager to arrive at the office each morning to see which patients were showing considerable improvement and getting well. Eventually, he left his clinic position and opened a private practice. He also became one of the instructors in orthomolecular therapy.

I have no doubt that if the few mental hospitals still in existence (some of which are being run by prisons) placed their patients on this orthomolecular program, they would find a major improvement in their patients over the years and a significant decrease in violent episodes.

I examined twelve of the most violent prisoners in the Prince Albert Penitentiary in northeast Saskatchewan many years ago. I found nine of them were chronic paranoid schizophrenics who were violent because, in most cases, they believed they had to defend themselves against their real or fancied enemies. One patient from this prison escaped and took two Royal Canadian Mounted Police officers as captives. He was eventually recaptured, and I saw him preparatory to his defense. He told me that he had to escape because the prison guard had decided to kill him. He "knew" this was true because he could smell the gas coming from the air vents. He tried repeatedly to plug the vent with clothes, to the annoyance of the staff. He "knew" they were also poisoning him because he could taste the bitter poison in his food, and he knew there was a plot because they were always talking about him. He was clearly schizophrenic. These schizophrenic prisoners need a treatment trial with the orthomolecular approach, but it is highly unlikely they will ever be treated adequately without it.

THE FUTURE FOR ORTHOMOLECULAR TREATMENT

When the first prominent institutions—medical colleges or research bodies—become interested and venturesome enough to test these claims and publish their results (assuming that they follow these protocols), there will a rush from all other curious centers to start using the orthomolecular approach. If and when orthomolecular therapy is widely accepted, the whole field of the biochemistry of schizophrenia and its treatment will flourish.

It would be very exciting to come back in the year 2020 to see what has happened to this field.

REFERENCES

1. Hoffer, A. Hoffer on Schizophrenia. Website http://www.islandnet.com/~hoffer/hofferhp.htm Members Mall, Health and Medicine, 1998.
2. Pauling, L. "Orthomolecular Psychiatry." *Science* 160: 265–271, 1968.
3. Pauling, L. "Orthomolecular Somatic and Psychiatric Medicine," *Sonderdruck aus den Zeitschrift Vitalstoffe—Zivilsationskrankeheiten* 12: 3–5, 1968.
4. Machlin, L. J. "Introduction," *Annals of the New York Academy of Sciences* 669: 1–6, 1992.
5. Altschul, R., Hoffer, A. and Stephen, J. D. "Influence of Nicotinic Acid on Serum Cholesterol in Man." *Archives of Biochemistry and Biophysics* 54: 558–559, 1955.

6. Conolly, J. *An Inquiry Concerning the Indications of Insanity (1830)*. London: Dawsons of Pall Mall, 1964.
7. Bleuler, Eugene. *Dementia Praecox or the Group of Schizophrenias*, 1911. Translated by J. Zinkin, New York: International Universities Press, 1950.
8. American Psychiatric Association. *Diagnostic Criteria from DSM-IV* Washington, D.C., 1994.
9. Hoffer, A. and Osmond, H. "A Card Sorting Test Helpful in Making Psychiatric Diagnosis." *Journal of Neuropsychiatry* 2: 306–330, 1961.
10. Hoffer, A., Kelm H., and Osmond, H. *The Hoffer-Osmond Diagnostic Test*. Huntington, New York: R. E. Krieger, 1975.
11. Hoffer Osmond Diagnostic Test Web Page http://www.islandnet.com Members Mall, Health and Medicine. Soft Tech. Ent., 1997.
12. El Meligi, A. M. and Osmond, H. *Experiential World Inventory. Manual for the Clinical Use of.* New York: Mens Sana Publishing, 1970. Available from R. Mullaly, Intuition Press, P.O. Box 404, Keene, N.H. 03431.
13. Hoffer, A., Osmond, H. and Smythies, J. "Schizophrenia: A New Approach, II: Results of a Year's Research." *Journal of Mental Science* 100: 29–45, 1954.
14. Hoffer, A. "Adrenochrome and Adrenolutin and Their Relationship to Mental Disease." *Psychotropic Drugs*, eds. S. Garattini and V. Ghetti, London: Elsevier Press, 10–20, 1957.
15. Hoffer, A. "The Adrenochrome Hypothesis of Schizophrenia Revisited." *Journal of Orthomolecular Psychiatry* 10: 98–118, 1981.
16. Hoffer, A. and Osmond, H. "The Adrenochrome Hypothesis and Psychiatry." *Journal of Orthomolecular Medicine* 5: 32–45, 1990.
17. Osmond, H. and Smythies, Journal of "Schizophrenia: A New Approach." *Journal of Mental Science* 98: 309–320, 1952.
18. Smythies, J. "On the Function of Neuromelanin." *Proceedings of the Royal Society* (London) B 263: 491–496, 1996.
19. Smythies, J. "The Role of Ascorbate in Brain: Therapeutic Implications." *Journal of the Royal Society of Medicine* 89: 241, 1996.
20. Smythies, J. "Disturbances of One-carbon Metabolism in Neuropsychiatric Disorders: A Review." *Biological Psychiatry* 41: 230–233, 1997.
21. Smythies, J. "Oxidative Reactions and Schizophrenia: A Review-discussion: *Schizophrenia Research* 24: 356–364, 1997.
22. Smythies, J. "Hallucinogenic Drugs." In *Encyclopedia of Neuroscience.* In press, 1997.

23. Hoffer, A. and Osmond, H. *The Hallucinogens*. New York, Academic Press, 1967.
24. Huxley, J., Mayr, E., Osmond, H. and Hoffer, A. "Schizophrenia as a Genetic Morphism." *Nature* 204: 220–221, 1964.
25. Hoffer, A. *Orthomolecular Medicine for Physicians*. Los Angeles, CA: Keats Publishing, 1989.
26. Hoffer, A. *Vitamin B-3 and Schizophrenia: Discovery, Recovery, Controversy*. Kingston, ON: Quarry Press, 1997, in press.
27. Kunin R. A. *Mega Nutrition. The New Prescription for Maximum Health, Energy and Longevity*. New York: McGraw Hill, 1980.
28. Cott, A., with J. Agel and E. Boc. *Dr Cott's Help for Your Learning Disabled Child: The Orthomolecular Treatment*. New York: Times Books, 1985.
29. Holford, P. *Mental Health. The Nutrition Connection: How to Enhance Your Mental Performance and Emotional Well Being*. On the other side: Pfeiffer, C. *How to Beat Depression, Anxiety and Schizophrenia*. London: Ion Press, 1996.
30. Hoffer, A. and Walker, M. *Orthomolecular Nutrition*. Los Angeles, CA: Keats Publishing, 1978.
31. Hoffer, A. and Walker, M. *Putting It All Together: The New Orthomolecular Nutrition*. Los Angeles, CA: Keats Publishing, 1996.
32. Hoffer, A. and Walker, M. *Smart Nutrients—A Guide to Nutrients That Can Prevent and Reverse Senility*. Garden City Park, NY: Avery Publishing Group, 1994.
33. Hoffer, A. *Hoffer's Law of Natural Nutrition*. Kingston, ON: Quarry Press, 1996.
34. Cott, A., "Controlled Fasting Treatment of Schizophrenia in USSR." *Schizophrenia* 3: 2–10, 1971.
35. Hoffer, A. *Vitamin B-3 (Niacin)*. Los Angeles, CA: Keats Publishing, 1984. Hoffer A. *Vitamin B-3 (Niacin) Update: New Roles for a Key Nutrient in Diabetes, Cancer, Heart Disease and Other Major Health Problems*. Los Angeles, CA: Keats Publishing, 1990.
36. Hoffer, A. "Safety, Side Effects and Relative Lack of Toxicity of Nicotinic Acid and Nicotinamide." *Schizophrenia* 1: 78–87, 1969.
37. Pfeiffer, C. C. *Mental and Elemental Nutrients*. Los Angeles, CA: Keats Publishing, 1975.
38. Hemila, H. "Does Vitamin C Alleviate the Symptoms of the Common Cold? A Review of Current Evidence." *Scandinavian Journal of Infectious Diseases* 26: 1–6, 1994.
39. DeLiz, A. J. "Large Amounts of Nicotinic Acid and Vitamin B-12 in the Treatment of Apparently Irreversible Psychotic

Conditions Found in Patients with Low Levels of Folic Acid." *Journal of Orthomolecular Psychiatry* 8: 63–65, 1979.

40. Simpson, L. O. "Capillary Blood Flow; Red Cell Shape: Implications for Clinical Haematology." *Advances in Physiological Fluid Dynamics*, ed. M. Singh and V. P. Saxena, New Delhi, India: Narosa Publishing House, 1995.

41. Simpson, L. O. "Chronic Tiredness and Idiopathic Chronic Fatigue—A Connection." *New Jersey Medicine* 89: 211–216, 1992.

42. Horrobin, D. F., Glen A. I. M. and Hudson C. J. "Possible Relevance of Phospholipid Abnormalities and Genetic Interactions in Psychiatric Disorders." *Medical Hypotheses* 45: 605–613, 1995.

43. Horrobin, D. F. "Schizophrenia: A Biochemical Disorder?" *Biomedicine* 32: 454–455, 1980.

44. Horrobin, D. F. "Schizophrenia as a Prostaglandin Deficiency Disease." *Lancet* 1: 936–937, 1977.

45. Horrobin, D. F. "Niacin Flushing, Prostaglandin E and Evening Primrose Oil: A Possible Objective Test for Monitoring Therapy in Schizophrenia." *Orthomolecular Psychiatry* 9: 33–34, 1980.

46. Rudin, D. and Felix, C., with Schrader, C. *The Omega-3 Phenomenon*. New York: Rawson Associates, 1987.

47. Rudin, D. O. "The Major Psychoses and Neuroses as Omega-3 Essential Fatty Acid Deficiency Syndrome: Substrate Pellagra." *Biological Psychiatry* 16: 837–850, 1981.

48. Rudin, D. O. "The Three Pellagras." *Journal of Orthomolecular Psychiatry* 12: 91–110, 1983.

49. Hoffer, A. and Mahon, M. "The Presence of Unidentified Substances in the Urine of Psychiatric Patients." *Journal of Neuropsychiatry* 2: 331–362, 1961.

50. Hoffer, A. and Osmond, H. "The Relationship Between an Unknown Factor (US) in Urine of Subjects and HOD Test Results." *Journal of Neuropsychiatry* 2: 363–368, 1961.

51. Pfeiffer, C. C. *Zinc and Other Micro-Nutrients*. Los Angeles, CA: Keats Publishing, 1978.

52. Pfeiffer, C. C. and LaMola S. "Zinc and Manganese in the Schizophrenias." *Journal of Orthomolecular Psychiatry* 12: 215–234, 1983.

53. Benton, D. and Cook, R. "The Impact of Selenium Supplementation on Mood." *Biological Psychiatry* 29: 1092–1098, 1991.

54. Foster, H. D. *Health, Disease & The Environment*. Boca Raton, FL: CRC Press, 1992.

55. Brown, J. S. and Foster, H. D. "Schizophrenia: An Update of

the Selenium Deficiency Hypothesis." *Journal of Orthomolecular Medicine* 11: 211–222, 1996.
56. Kunin, R. A. "Manganese and Niacin in the Treatment of Drug-induced Dyskinesias." *Journal of Orthomolecular Psychiatry* 5: 4–27, 1976.
57. Hawkins, D. R. "The Prevention of Tardive Dyskinesia with High Dosage Vitamins: A Study of 58,000 Patients." *Journal of Orthomolecular Medicine* 1: 24–26, 1986.
58. Kunin, R. A. *Syllabus of Orthomolecular Laboratory Usage.* San Francisco, CA: Society for Orthomolecular Health-Medicine, 1997.
59. Pauling, L. *How To Live Longer and Feel Better.* New York: W. H. Freeman & Co. 1986.
60. Hoffer, A. *Niacin Therapy in Psychiatry.* Springfield, IL: C. C. Thomas, 1962.
61. Horrobin, D. "Niacin Skin Flush in Schizophrenia." *Schizophrenia Research.* [He summarized this research at the Canadian Schizophrenia Foundation Twenty-Sixth Annual Meeting, Toronto, 1997.]
62. Horrobin, D. *Nutritional Management of Nerve Damage in Diabetes, Attention Deficit Disorder and Dyslexia.* Twenty-sixth Annual International Conference, International Society for Orthomolecular Medicine, Toronto, 1997.
63. Ward, P., Sutherland, J., Glen, E., Glen, A. I. M., and Horrobin, D. F. "Skin Flushing in Response to Graded Doses of Topical Niacin: A New Test Which Distinguishes Schizophrenics from Controls." *Schizophrenia Research,* 24: 70, 1997.
64. Hoffer, A., Osmond, H., Callbeck, M. J. and Kahan, I. "Treatment of Schizophrenia with Nicotinic Acid and Nicotinamide." *Journal of Clinical Experimental Psychopathology* 18: 131–158, 1957.
65. Hoffer, A. and Osmond, H. *The Chemical Basis of Clinical Psychiatry.* Springfield, IL: C. C. Thomas, 1960.
66. Osmond, H. and Hoffer, A. "Massive Niacin Treatment in Schizophrenia: Review of a Nine-year Study." *Lancet* 1: 316–320, 1963.
67. Hoffer, A. and Osmond, H. *How to Live with Schizophrenia.* New York, NY: University Books, 1966. (Also published by Johnson, London, 1966.) Revised edition, New York: Citadel Press, 1992. New edition, fall 1997.
68. Osmond, H., and Hoffer, A., "Schizophrenia and Suicide," *Journal of Schizophrenia* 1: 54–64, 1967.
69. Hoffer, A. "Five California Schizophrenics." *Journal of Schizophrenia* 1: 209–220, 1967.

70. Hoffer, A. "Treatment of Schizophrenia with a Therapeutic Program Based upon Nicotinic Acid as the Main Variable," *Molecular Basis of Some Aspects of Mental Activity, vol II.,* ed. O. Walaas, New York: Academic Press, 1967.

71. Hoffer, A. "Mechanism of Action of Nicotinic Acid and Nicotinamide in the Treatment of Schizophrenia." In *Orthomolecular Psychiatry,* ed. D. R. Hawkins and Linus Pauling. San Francisco: W. H. Freeman and Co., 1973.

72. Hoffer, A. "Natural History and Treatment of Thirteen Pairs of Identical Twins, Schizophrenic and Schizophrenic-spectrum conditions." *Journal of Orthomolecular Psychiatry* 5: 101–122, 1976.

73. Hoffer, A. and Osmond H., "Schizophrenia: Another Long-Term Follow-up in Canada." *Journal of Orthomolecular Psychiatry* 9: 107–113, 1980.

74. Hoffer, A. "Orthomolecular Medicine." In *Molecules In Natural Science and Medicine, An Encomium for Linus Pauling.* Ed. Z. B. Maksic and M. Eckert-Maksic, Chichester, England: Ellis Horwood Ltd., 1991.

75. Millar, T. P. "The Revolving Door Is Stuck on Out." *The Medical Post,* May 20, 1997.

76. Hoffer, A., "Chronic Schizophrenic Patients Treated Ten Years or More." *Journal of Orthomolecular Medicine* 9: 7–37, 1994.

Printed in the USA
CPSIA information can be obtained
at www.ICGtesting.com
JSHW011012280723
45560JS00005B/181